2.95

Carme Solé Vendrell
Josep M. Parramón

Summer

elair
PUBLISHING COMPANY INC.

When the sun is happy...

... and the fields are full of colors...

... and fruit ripens...

... and stores close...

When people travel...

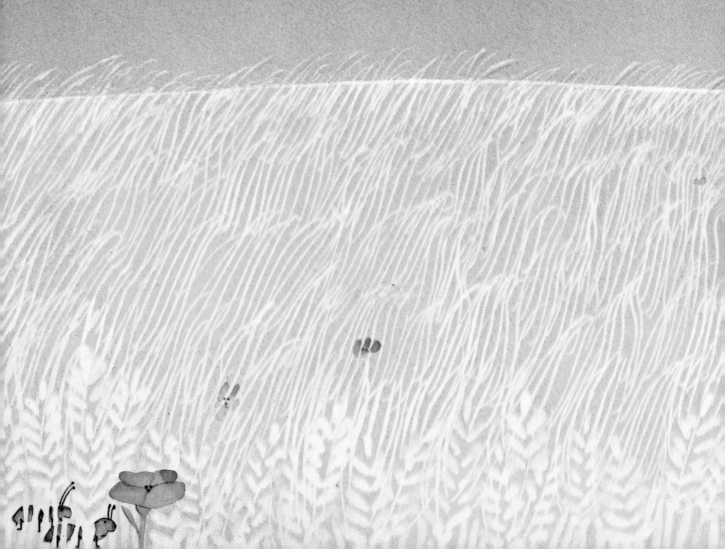

... and wheat
is the color of gold...

... and the sun is redder...

... and children
go to the beach...

... and boats go to sea...

When everyone
is very thirsty...

... and it is very hot...

It's summer!

SUMMER

The shortest night of the year

Two days after the beginning of summer the sun reaches its highest point in the sky. That day is the longest day of the year and the night is the shortest night.

The sun grows warmer, fruits ripen.

In July, August, and September, as the sun grows warmer, more fruits ripen. First come the strawberries, then the cherries, apricots, and plums, followed by the pears, watermelons, cantaloupes, and finally the grapes. What lovely desserts!

Schools close; it's vacation time.

Summer vacation usually begins in June – almost three months with no school, no getting up early, no books! But good students keep learning in summer.

Stores close, people travel.

Many small stores close for a few days during the summer so the people who work in them can rest. Many people travel by car or train or boat or plane. They get to know new places and new people.

But in the country this is a time for work.

The harvest of wheat begins in summer. The farmers work with a big machine that cuts and gathers the wheat and separates the wheat from the straw. Wheat is one of our most important foods. From wheat we make bread and cereal, spaghetti and cakes!

Summer is the hottest month of the year.

Yes, it is very hot and the children and adults dress in light, bright-colored clothes. Those who live near the ocean go swimming at the beach, those who live in the mountains, swim in lakes, rivers, and pools. But everyone is hot. People eat ice cream cones and take cool drinks.

But Summer is healthy and happy.

During the summer we go to the country, we go to the ocean, we go out in the sun; we eat fruit and drink more water; we stay outdoors. This is better, more fun, and healthier. Three cheers for the sun! Three cheers for summer.